Learning to read. Reading to learn!

LEVEL ONE Sounding It Out Preschool–Kindergarten
For kids who know their alphabet and are starting to sound out words.

learning sight words • beginning reading • sounding out words

LEVEL TWO Reading with Help Preschool–Grade 1
For kids who know sight words and are learning to sound out new words.

expanding vocabulary • building confidence • sounding out bigger words

LEVEL THREE Independent Reading Grades 1–3
For kids who are beginning to read on their own.

introducing paragraphs • challenging vocabulary • reading for comprehension

LEVEL FOUR Chapters Grades 2–4
For confident readers who enjoy a mixture of images and story.

reading for learning • more complex content • feeding curiosity

Ripley Readers Designed to help kids build their reading skills and
confidence at any level, this program offers a variety of fun, entertaining, and
unbelievable topics to interest even the most reluctant readers. With stories and
information that will spark their curiosity, each book will motivate them to start
and keep reading.

PUBLISHING

Vice President, Licensing & Publishing   Amanda Joiner
Editorial Manager   Carrie Bolin

Editor   Jordie R. Orlando
Writer   Korynn Wible-Freels
Designer   Scott Swanson
Reprographics   Bob Prohaska
Production Design   Luis Fuentes

Published by Ripley Publishing 2021

10 9 8 7 6 5 4 3 2 1

Copyright © 2021 Ripley Publishing

ISBN: 978-1-60991-404-2

No part of this publication may be reproduced in whole or in part, stored in a retrieval system, or transmitted in any form by any means, electronic, mechanical, photocopying, recording, or otherwise, without written permission from the publisher.

For more information regarding permission, contact:
VP Licensing & Publishing
Ripley Entertainment Inc.
7576 Kingspointe Parkway, Suite 188
Orlando, Florida 32819

Email: publishing@ripleys.com
www.ripleys.com/books
Manufactured in China in May 2020.

First Printing

Library of Congress Control Number:
2020937133

PUBLISHER'S NOTE
While every effort has been made to verify the accuracy of the entries in this book, the Publisher cannot be held responsible for any errors contained in the work. They would be glad to receive any information from readers.

Ripley Readers

Crazy Cars!

All true and unbelievable!

Ripley
PUBLISHING

a Jim Pattison Company

Come and see these neat rides!

This car is
so little!

Only one person
can fit in it!

Did you see that car go by?

It is the fastest one in the world!

Look! That car can go in the water!

Do you want to take a ride in this shoe?

It must have taken a long time to make a car from matchsticks!

A car that looks like food!

Do you like bananas?

Have you seen this fish car
that plays music?

How funny!

Wow! That car is so pretty!

Blast off!

Do not stand too close
to this truck!

It took twelve miles of red yarn
to make this ride!

Do you play with LEGO?

Have you made something this big?

Can you think up a new ride?

Ready for More?

Ripley Readers feature unbelievable but true facts and stories!

LEVEL ONE
Sounding it out

LEVEL TWO
Reading with help

LEVEL THREE
Independent reading

LEVEL FOUR
Chapters

Bears!

Caves!

Animal Imposters!

Take Flight!

Sports!

Raging Raptors!

Odd Ocean!

Mythical Creatures!

For more information about Ripley's Believe It or Not!, go to www.ripleys.com